Scientific Discovery in the Renaissance

By Stacia Deutsch and Rhody Cohon

TABLE OF CONTENTS

INTRODUCTION	2
CHAPTER 1 Breakthroughs in Medicine	4
CHAPTER 2 Breakthroughs in Math and Engineering	12
CHAPTER 3 Breakthroughs in Astronomy	20
CONCLUSION	28
SOLVE THIS ANSWERS	30
GLOSSARY	31
INDEX	32

Introduction

A great change began in Italy and slowly spread across Europe from about the mid-1300s through the 1600s. This time period became known as the Renaissance (REH-nih-zahns). *Renaissance* is a French word meaning **revival**, a renewed interest in something from the past. Many men and women who lived during the Renaissance studied art and culture from ancient Rome and Greece. Then, they adapted those old ideas to their lives.

The Renaissance was a period of change. In the past, church leaders controlled much of what people thought and believed. But during the Renaissance, people were eager to explore the world for themselves. Artists painted and sculpted great works of art.

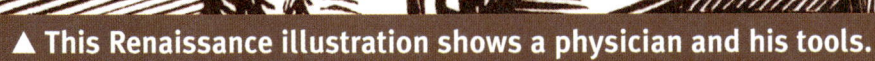
▲ This Renaissance illustration shows a physician and his tools.

Writers penned poems, letters, and stories. Musicians wrote new songs.

Some of the greatest changes happened in science. Even though the word *scientist* did not exist during the Renaissance, scholars were busy studying the physical world. They did experiments and recorded what happened. They observed animal behavior and daily life. Some scholars studied the stars and movement of the planets. They also used principles of math to learn new things about the natural world.

Read on to learn about the amazing science discoveries of the Renaissance. You will see how four-hundred-year-old scientific ideas continue to affect us today.

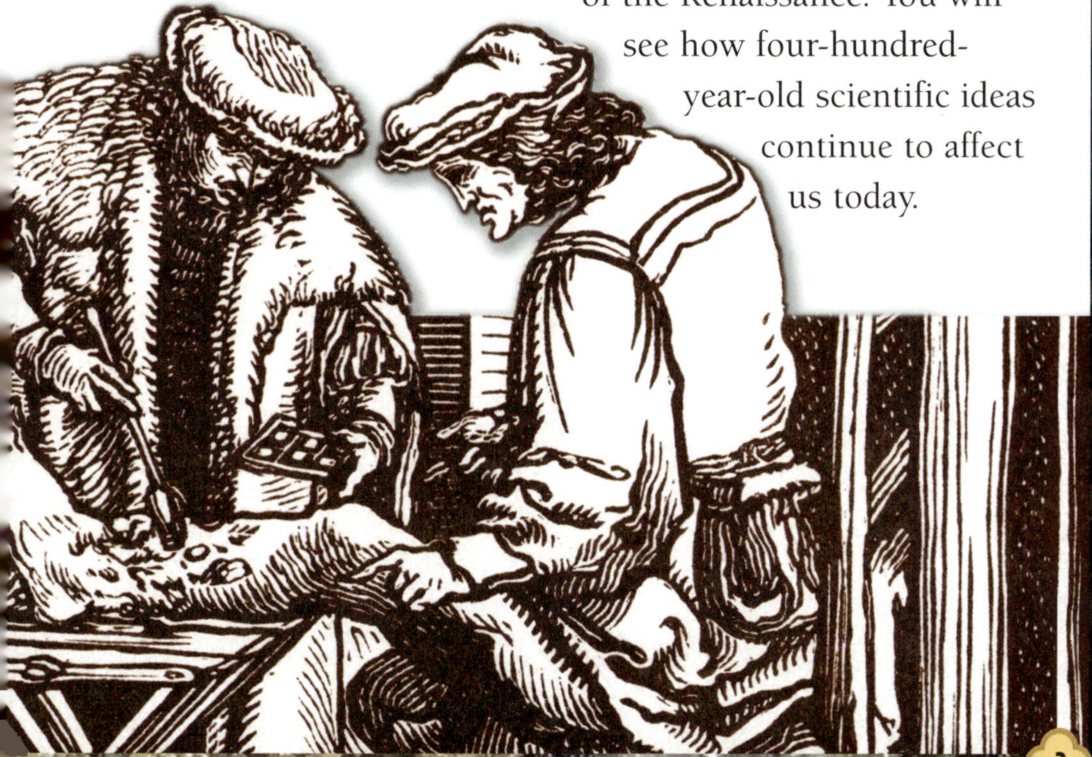

▲ **The Renaissance began in Italy and then spread through Europe.**

Chapter 1

Breakthroughs in Medicine

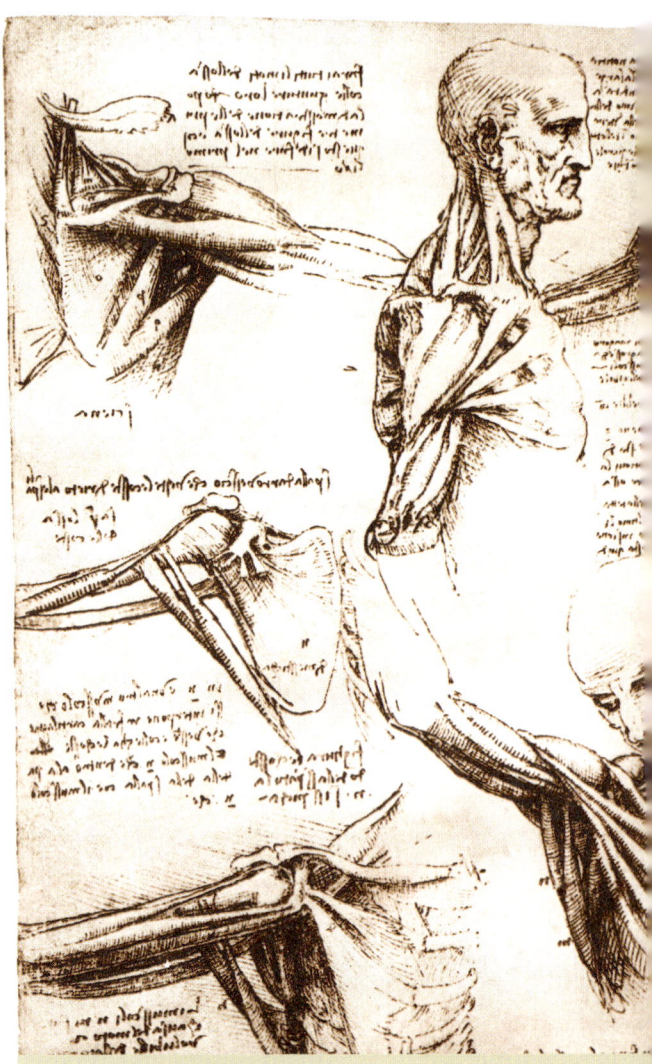

One of the most famous artists of the Renaissance also learned many important things about science. Leonardo da Vinci, known for painting *The Mona Lisa*, studied medicine and the human body.

Artists during the Renaissance wanted to show the human form with the most exact details possible. Leonardo da Vinci wanted to understand what was under a person's skin. He wanted to know about bone structure and how muscles worked.

▲ Leonardo da Vinci invented a way of drawing multiple views, or cross sections of the body. Cross sections are widely used in scientific studies today.

Even though he wasn't a doctor, da Vinci was a leader in **anatomy**, the study of the human body. Around 1510, a local hospital allowed da Vinci to cut apart the bodies of dead patients for study. He studied more than thirty bodies, and measured and sketched what he saw.

When he died, da Vinci left behind thousands of drawings. More than 200 of them were drawings of anatomy.

Sadly, da Vinci never shared his work with others. No one knew about his studies of anatomy until long after the Renaissance.

1. SOLVE THIS

Many Renaissance scholars used the work of a man named Fibonacci (fee-boh-NAH-chee). Fibonacci developed a famous way of adding numbers in a sequence. The sequence relates to patterns found in nature. The Fibonacci Sequence is: 1, 1, 2, 3, 5, 8, 13 . . . What would be the next number in the series?

MATH ✔ POINT

Explain what steps you followed to get your answer.

IT'S A FACT

Leonardo da Vinci was called the "Universal Man." In addition to painting and anatomy, he studied architecture, science, astronomy, sculpting, geology, and engineering. He even imagined and sketched an early helicopter.

▲ da Vinci's helicopter

CHAPTER 1

Anatomy

Unlike da Vinci, many scholars wanted to share their ideas. About 1450, the printing press was invented in Germany. The press made it possible to produce many copies of a book by machine. Before, people had to write each book by hand. Now scholars were able to write about their work and read about other people's discoveries. This helped them build on the research of others.

Andreas Vesalius (ahn-DRAY-uhs veh-SAY-lee-uhs) (1514–1564) lived in Belgium. He was the first to publish his own research of the human body. Many people read his seven-book series and became interested in studying anatomy, too.

◄ Vesalius's book, *De Humani Corporis Fabrica* (*On the Fabric of the Human Body*), was used as a textbook for training doctors. This is a drawing of the muscle system.

BREAKTHROUGHS IN MEDICINE

A man named Hieronymus Fabricius (huh-ROH-nih-muhs FAH-bree-kuhs) studied blood. Fabricius discovered that there are one-way valves in blood veins. But he never understood what the valves were for.

In England, William Harvey studied Fabricius's theories. Harvey found out that the valves move blood in only one direction. He also discovered that blood is pumped through the heart. The work of these scientists led to new medicines and better treatments for disease.

▲ William Harvey

EVERYDAY SCIENCE

William Harvey found that blood flows in only one direction. Try this: Hang your hand down by your side. Watch the veins fill with blood. They may swell slightly. Press on one of the veins. The vein will disappear as the blood stops flowing through it. When you let go, the vein will refill with blood.

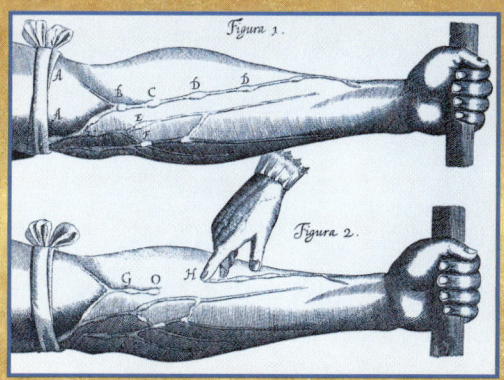

▲ Valves in our veins prevent our blood from running backward.

CHAPTER 1

Medicine

Before the Renaissance, nearly half of all babies died shortly after being born. About 25 million people died from the Bubonic plague. Renaissance doctors needed to create new medicines. They wanted to prevent diseases from spreading.

Apothecaries (uh-PAH-thuh-cair-eez) were people who made medicines during the Renaissance. They experimented with plants brought back to Europe by explorers. In Cuba, tobacco was used as a medicine. On his second voyage, Christopher Columbus brought home tobacco seeds.

▲ This engraving of a French pharma was done in 1624.

CAREERS

A naturopath is a doctor who prescribes natural remedies, or treatments, made of plants and herbs, just like physicians did 400 years ago. Instead of chemical-based medicines and surgery, a naturopath follows a natural approach to healing.

BREAKTHROUGHS IN MEDICINE

Ferdinand Magellan was a Portuguese explorer. He was the first to sail around the world. He brought back spices and plants to use as medicines.

Some plants used to make medicines include rosemary, thyme, mint, lavender, and roses. Some medicines of the time worked and others did not. Renaissance apothecaries learned about how our bodies react to many different kinds of medicine. Their work opened the door for future experiments.

2. SOLVE THIS

It took Magellan's crew three years to complete their voyage. If a modern satellite takes ninety minutes to circle Earth, how many times would a satellite orbit Earth in three years?

MATH ✓ POINT

What steps did you follow to get your answer?

Ferdinand Magellan ▶

CHAPTER 1

Medical Schools

The first medical schools in Europe were in hospitals. In the late Renaissance, public dissections helped doctors train. Surgeons gathered around a body and cut into it for research. Then they developed new techniques.

There were no trained physicians in many towns and villages. Local barbers performed surgery. We couldn't imagine going to a barber for surgery, but some of these barber-surgeons added to the advances in medicine.

3. SOLVE THIS

The average human man has 5 quarts of blood in his body. If 5 quarts equals 4.7 liters, how many quarts are there in one liter of blood?

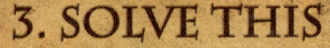

Does your answer seem reasonable to you?

▲ Dissections were often performed in theater-like arenas.

BREAKTHROUGHS IN MEDICINE

Ambroise Paré (AHM-brohz pahr-AY) was a French doctor who developed many new ways to treat patients. He was the first to use false teeth, artificial limbs, and eyes made of gold and silver.

He also wanted to find a kinder way to treat patients. Before Paré, most surgeons poured boiling oil over a wound to seal it shut. Paré developed a gentle mixture of eggs and turpentine. His mixture seemed to heal better and hurt less.

◀ Ambroise Paré

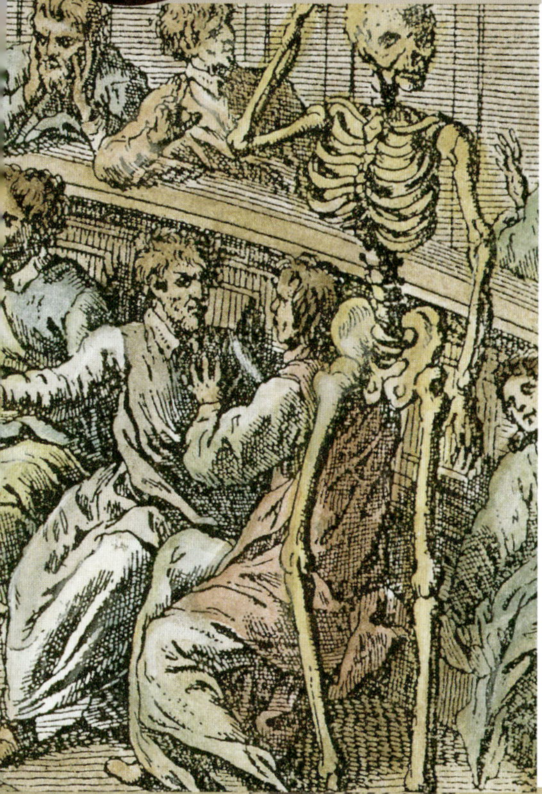

HISTORICAL PERSPECTIVE

Renaissance doctors used blood-sucking animals called leeches to drain poisons from a person's body. Some doctors still use leeches to prevent blood from clotting during surgery.

▲ Some doctors still use leeches today.

11

Chapter 2

Breakthroughs in Math and Engineering

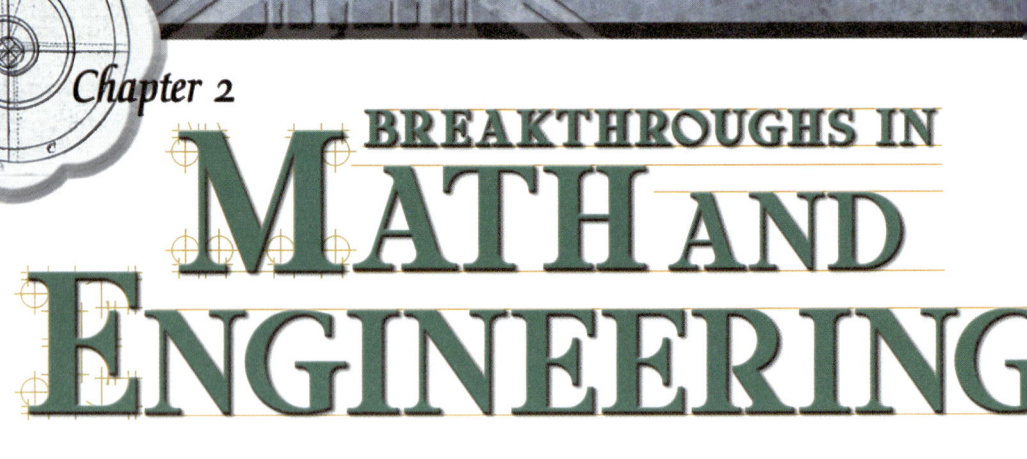

Renaissance scholars applied mathematics to everything from art to astronomy. Drawings used to be two-dimensional, or flat. These new thinkers found ways to draw in three dimensions. In a three-dimensional painting, some objects appear to be nearby and others seem far away. This is called **perspective**.

Filippo Brunelleschi (fee-LEE-poh broo-neh-LEHS-kee) was the leader in perspective drawing. Italian-born Brunelleschi was both an architect and engineer.

They Made A Difference
Leon Battista Alberti

Leon Battista Alberti (LEE-ahn bah-TEES-tah al-BAIR-tee) devised a grid to help an artist use math to figure out the distances needed to create perspective. A grid is a square network of evenly spaced horizontal and vertical lines. Alberti's grid was made of black thread and attached to a wooden frame.

He used principles of math to help him with perspective drawing. He often applied **symmetry** and **ratios** to his work. Symmetry is when two sides of a design are exactly the same. Ratios are used to find proportional, or size, relationships between objects. Symmetry and ratios were commonly used in Greek and Roman art and architecture.

Brunelleschi used both of these ideas to determine a **vanishing point.** The vanishing point is the place where two lines come together. It gives the appearance of space and distance.

This portrait of Brunelleschi ▶ is a good example of the two-dimensional drawing he helped to transform.

CHAPTER 2

Architecture

Brunelleschi studied examples of Greek and Roman architecture, such as the Pantheon in Rome. He used mathematical perspective to do his own designs. His most famous creation is the Dome of the Florence Cathedral in Italy, also known as the Duomo (DWOH-moh). The Duomo was completed in 1436.

The dome was built without a supporting frame. Brunelleschi had to convince the authorities that his design would not cave in. He used principles of math and engineering to make his case.

▲ The Duomo was the largest domed building erected since the Pantheon in Rome was built between 27 B.C. and A.D. 128.

BREAKTHROUGHS IN MATH AND ENGINEERING

EYEWITNESS ACCOUNT

"The object of his [Brunelleschi's] architectural researches, however, was not to learn to reproduce Roman architecture, but to enrich the architecture of his own time and to perfect his engineering skills."

—famous artist Donatello about his friend Brunelleschi

Brunelleschi's dome was 295.8 feet (91.2 meters) from the roof of the church to the highest point. Two years after Brunelleschi finished the large dome, a **cupola** (KYOO-puh-luh), a second small dome, was added on top. This increased the top to 375.7 feet (114.5 meters) tall.

Today, a visitor can climb the 463 steps to the top of the Duomo to enjoy an incredible view of Florence. This is a similar view to the one Brunelleschi's craftspeople experienced hundreds of years ago.

▲ Symmetry and ratios were used to build many Renaissance buildings.

4. SOLVE THIS

The Duomo's incredible diameter of 130 feet (39.6 meters) was smaller than the diameter of the Pantheon in Rome. The Duomo's diameter was 91.5 percent of the Pantheon's. What was the Pantheon's diameter in feet?

MATH ✓ POINT

What steps did you take to arrive at the answer?

CHAPTER 2

Mapmaking

Renaissance explorers Christopher Columbus and Ferdinand Magellan had proven that Earth was round. Now, explorers needed maps that could show the round Earth on flat paper.

In 1569, Gerard Mercator (muhr-KAY-tuhr), a Belgian **cartographer** (kahr-TAH-gruh-fuhr), studied the use of perspective. A cartographer is someone who makes maps. Mercator drew a grid of lines that ran across an entire map.

These lines were called latitude and longitude.

▼ The famous "Mercator's Perspective" map is still used today.

◀ Gerard Mercator

BREAKTHROUGHS IN MATH AND ENGINEERING

They represented spherical coordinates for finding any location on Earth. His map was a masterpiece. It was called "Mercator's Perspective." The map was huge, covering eighteen large panels.

Mercator's grid system is still the basis of modern mapmaking. Mapmakers still use his map to create marine charts. However, to make new maps, mapmakers today rely on digital photographs provided by satellites.

5. SOLVE THIS

The longest distance around Earth is the equator. Earth at the equator measures about 24,902 miles (40,075.8 kilometers). How far is it to the center of Earth?

MATH ✓ POINT

What formula did you need to solve the question?

THEY MADE A DIFFERENCE
Georgius Agricola

Georgius Agricola (jor-JEE-oo uh-GREE-kuh-luh) was a German physician and scientist. He is known as the father of mineralogy. He was a pioneer in physical geology and the first to classify minerals scientifically. His book *De re metallica* was a standard in metallurgy for more than 100 years.

▲ woodcut of a water-powered pump of Agricola

CHAPTER 2

Physics

Some scholars used math ideas to create art and architecture. Other scholars used math to study how objects move. This is called **physics**. Physics experiments during the Renaissance led to some exciting discoveries.

▲ It is a myth that Galileo conducted physics experiments by dropping cannonballs off the side of the Leaning Tower of Pisa.

BREAKTHROUGHS IN MATH AND ENGINEERING

The best-recorded experiments came from the Italian Galileo Galilei (gah-luh-LAY-oh gah-luh-LAY). Galileo tracked falling objects. He dropped different things from great heights and measured how long it took them to hit the ground. He discovered that all objects have the same speed of acceleration, no matter what their weights are.

William Gilbert (England, 1544–1603) was a metallurgist. He studied the properties of metals. He was the first to discover the properties of **lodestone** (LOHD-stohn), magnetic iron ore. His book *De Magnete* detailed his findings about magnets, compasses, and Earth's magnetic pull. *De Magnete* influenced some of Galileo's ideas.

Scholars did many physics experiments during the Renaissance. They studied acceleration, magnetism, spin, and **trajectory** (truh-JEHK-tuh-ree). Trajectory is the arc, or path, an object takes as it flies through the air. These experiments led to a revolution in ideas regarding the planets and how they move.

◀ Lodestone is a rare magnetic iron ore that acts like a magnet.

Chapter 3

BREAKTHROUGHS IN
ASTRONOMY

Before the Renaissance, powerful leaders of the church decided what people learned. The church taught that Earth was at the center of the universe. The sun, stars, and planets circled around Earth. During the Renaissance, astronomers questioned this belief.

The Polish scientist Nicolaus Copernicus (NIH-koh-luhs kuh-PUHR-nih-kuhs) watched the skies and recorded his observations. Using mathematics, he determined that the sun, not Earth, is the center of our solar system. This is called the **heliocentric** (hee-lee-oh-SEHN-trihk) theory. *Helio* means "sun" in Latin. *Centric* means centered.

▲ Nicolaus Copernicus

Copernicus then ordered the planets by the length of their orbit around the sun.

▲ **This is the diagram of the solar system Copernicus had in his book.**

He spent thirty years on his study of the planets. Everything Copernicus observed went against what the church was teaching. He was afraid to publish his observations. In fact, he died a few hours after he held the first copy of his book, *De Revolutionibus Orbium Coelestium*. In English, this means *On the Revolutions of the Celestial Orbs*.

Copernicus's work was all theory. He never found solid proof that Earth orbited the sun. However, he left such detailed work that other Renaissance astronomers eventually proved him correct.

CHAPTER 3

Heliocentric Confirmations

Galileo Galilei studied both physics and astronomy. Galileo agreed with Copernicus's heliocentric theory. He invented the first telescope.

With his telescope, the stars and planets appeared thirty times larger. Galileo discovered four moons revolving around Jupiter. From this, Galileo understood that everything was not circling Earth.

▲ Galileo invented the first telescope.

◀ Galileo

BREAKTHROUGHS IN ASTRONOMY

✓POINT THINK ABOUT IT

Galileo produced the first scientific evidence supporting the heliocentric theory. Finally someone had proven Copernicus was right.

Galileo boldly published his findings. Church leaders put him on trial for going against their teachings. He was forced to retract, or withdraw, his claims.

At the end of his trial, Galileo was sentenced to house arrest for the rest of his life. He quietly said, "Nevertheless, it does move." What do you think he was referring to?

▲ Galileo shows his telescopic discovery of the satellites of Jupiter in 1610.

CHAPTER 3

Planetary Motion

The Catholic Church's authority did not reach as far as Denmark. There, Tycho Brahe (TY-koh BRAH) studied astronomy without fear of being arrested. He watched the stars, carefully measuring and recording their positions in the sky. Then, he created a catalog of more than 1,000 stars. It was not the first or largest star catalog, but it was the most accurate.

▲ Danish astronomer Tycho Brahe

BREAKTHROUGHS IN ASTRONOMY

In 1600, German Johannes Kepler (yoh-HAH-nuhs KEHP-luhr) became Brahe's assistant. Kepler calculated the most accurate astronomy tables known. These tables supported Copernicus's and Galileo's theories of heliocentric astronomy.

Kepler did not just study astronomy. He also did experiments with optics (light) and geometric shapes. For his work, in 1601, Kepler was made the Imperial Mathematician to Emperor Rudolf of Prague.

THEY MADE A DIFFERENCE
Sophia Brahe

Sophia Brahe, the daughter of Tycho, was a well-known researcher in her own right. She helped her father with his planetary observations. She also studied horticulture, the science of plants and flowers. Some of her research methods are still in use in universities today.

◀ Johannes Kepler

CHAPTER 3

Kepler is most widely remembered for outlining the three laws of planetary motion. He believed that the planetary system could be explained with mathematics. This was a very unusual idea. Even with all the new scientific discoveries, Renaissance scholars simply did not understand many things. They would say that certain things were mysterious or simply "unknown."

Kepler created complex mathematical calculations to explain what he observed in the skies. He kept careful records. Over time, he determined that there were three common laws of planetary motion.

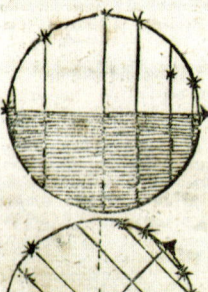
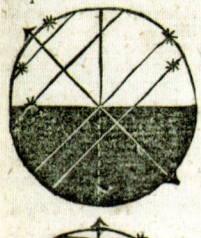
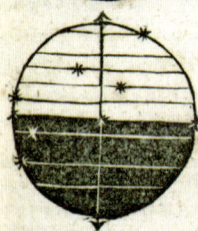

▲ On Brahe's deathbed, Kepler promised to complete a table based on Tycho's observations.

BREAKTHROUGHS IN ASTRONOMY

1. Planets orbit in ellipses, not circles as had been commonly thought.
2. A planet moves more quickly when along the part of the ellipse that has a shorter radius. The farther the planet is from the sun, the more slowly it moves along its orbit.
3. The period of a planet's orbit, or time it takes to orbit the sun, is proportional to its distance from the sun.

These three laws had a huge impact during the Renaissance. Even today, astronomers and astronauts continue to study Kepler's laws.

 POINT
TALK ABOUT IT IT

Who is your favorite "hero" from this book? Why? How has this Renaissance scientist impacted science today?

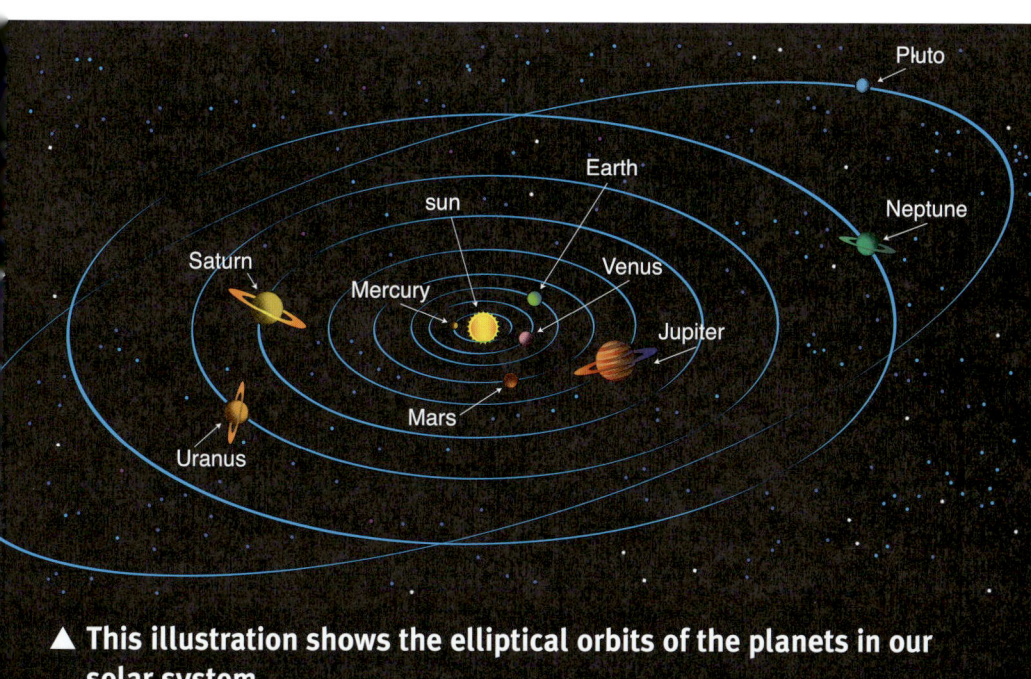

▲ This illustration shows the elliptical orbits of the planets in our solar system.

27

Conclusion

The Renaissance changed the study of science forever. Scholars carefully observed the world. They performed experiments, recorded results, and applied principles of math to what they saw. Their research brought about breakthroughs in medicine and astronomy, as well as in math and engineering.

Some of the scholars' names are familiar, like da Vinci, Brunelleschi, and Columbus. Others we speak of less frequently, but the work of all of them continues to inspire us today.

▲ This is the Copernicus crater on the moon.

1436 — Brunelleschi completes the Duomo.

1500 — Columbus completes his third trip to the New World, bringing home plant samples for use as medicines.

1519 — Da Vinci dies, leaving behind more than 600 studies of anatomy.

1543 — Vesalius publishes his seven-book study of the human body, which changes the way doctors treat patients. Copernicus publishes his heliocentric theory and dies a few hours later.

Some scholars are honored in our modern scientific world. NASA, the United States National Aeronautics and Space Administration, pays tribute to Renaissance astronomers.

A crater on the moon is called Copernicus. The *Galileo* spacecraft was launched in 1989. In 2008, NASA will launch a satellite on a mission called the Kepler Mission.

Leonardo da Vinci said, "There shall be wings! If the accomplishment be not for me, 'tis for some other." We thank the scholars of the Renaissance for taking risks, sharing their knowledge, and propelling us boldly into the future.

▲ NASA named this spacecraft after Galileo. *Galileo* is the first spacecraft that went to Jupiter.

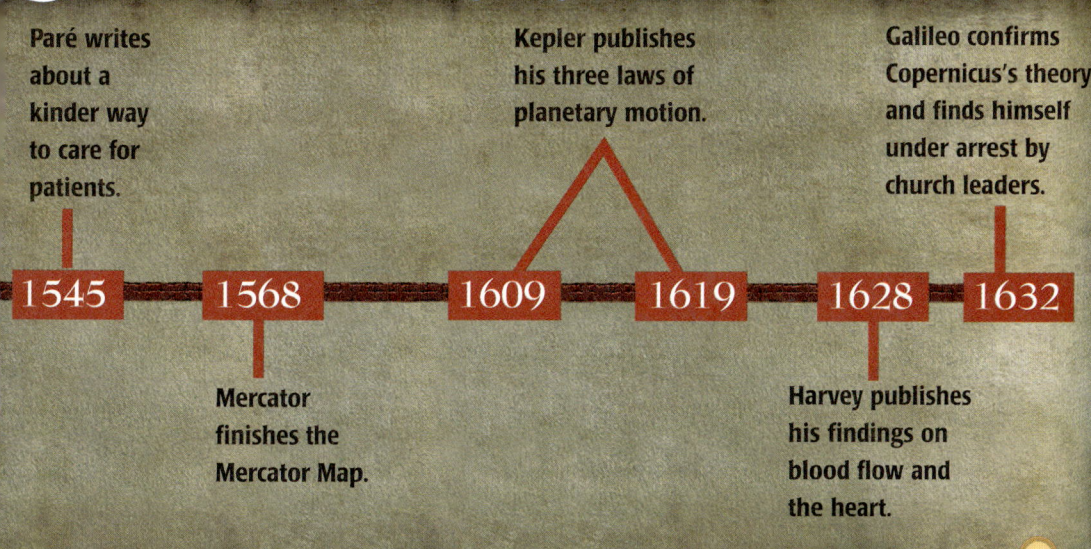

Paré writes about a kinder way to care for patients. — 1545

Mercator finishes the Mercator Map. — 1568

Kepler publishes his three laws of planetary motion. — 1609 — 1619

Galileo confirms Copernicus's theory and finds himself under arrest by church leaders. — 1628

Harvey publishes his findings on blood flow and the heart. — 1632

SOLVE THIS
Answers

1. Page 5 21 (Add together the two previous numbers in the series.)

    8 + 13 = 21

2. Page 9 17,520

    365 days x 24 hours/day x 3 years = 26,280 hours in 3 years

    90 minutes = 1.5 hours

    26,280 / 1.5 = 17,520 trips around the world in 3 years

3. Page 10 1.06 quarts = 1 liter (5 / 4.7)

4. Page 15 142 feet (43.3 meters)

    130 feet = .915x (x = the unknown diameter of the Pantheon)

    130 / .915 = 142

    (39.6 meters = .915x

    39.6 / .915 = 43.3)

5. Page 17 3,965.3 miles (6,377.4 kilometers)

    circumference = pi x 2 x radius

    24,902 = 3.14 x 2 x radius

    24,902 / (3.14 x 2) = radius

    3,965.3 = radius

    (40,075.8 = 3.142 x 2 x radius

    40,075.8 / (3.142 x 2) = radius

    6,377.4 = radius)

GLOSSARY

anatomy (uh-NAH-tuh-mee) the study of the human body (page 5)

apothecary (uh-PAH-thuh-cair-ee) person who made medicines; pharmacist (page 8)

cartographer (kahr-TAH-gruh-fuhr) mapmaker (page 16)

cupola (KYOO-puh-luh) a small dome (page 15)

heliocentric (hee-lee-oh-SEHN-trihk) sun-centered (page 20)

lodestone (LOHD-stohn) a stone with iron in it that acts as a magnet (page 19)

perspective (puhr-SPEHK-tihv) a way of drawing that makes pictures look three-dimensional (page 12)

physics (FIH-zihks) the mathematical, scientific study of matter and energy and how objects move (page 18)

ratio (RAY-shee-oh) a comparison of two quantities or numbers using division; ratios are usually expressed as fractions (page 13)

revival (rih-VY-vuhl) to bring something back into use (page 2)

symmetry (SIH-muh-tree) a balanced arrangement of parts on either side of a line or around a central point (page 13)

trajectory (truh-JEHK-tuh-ree) the arc of a flying object (page 19)

vanishing point (VAH-nihsh-ihng POINT) point where lines come together used to give a picture perspective (page 13)

Index

anatomy, 5–6, 28
apothecaries, 8–9
architecture, 5, 13–15, 18
art, 2–3, 13, 18
astronomy, 20–28
Brahe, Sophie, 25
Brahe, Tycho, 24–26
Brunelleschi, Filippo, 12–15, 28
cartographer, 16
Columbus, Christopher, 8, 16, 28
Copernicus, Nicolaus, 20–23, 25, 28–29
cupola, 15
da Vinci, Leonardo, 4–6, 28–29
Duomo, 14–15, 28
Fabricius, Hieronymus, 7
Galilei, Galileo, 18–19, 22–23, 25, 29
Harvey, William, 7, 29
heliocentric, 20, 22, 25, 28

Kepler, Johannes, 25–27, 29
Laws of Planetary Motion, 24, 26–27, 29
lodestone, 19
Magellan, Ferdinand, 9, 16
mapmaking, 16–17
mathematics, 3, 12–14, 17, 20, 25–26, 28
medicine, 4, 7–9, 11, 28
Mercator, Gerard, 16–17, 29
Paré, Ambroise, 11, 29
perspective, 12–14, 16–17
physics, 18–19, 22
ratio, 13, 15
revival, 2
symmetry, 13, 15
trajectory, 19
vanishing point, 13
Vesalius, Andreas, 6, 28